A Journeyof
Healing

A Journeyof
Healing

What Every Woman Should Know About Breast Cancer

Elizabeth Arredondo MEd, LPC-S

Trilogy Christian Publishers A Wholly Owned Subsidiary of Trinity Broadcasting Network 2442 Michelle Drive Tustin, CA 92780

Copyright © 2021 Elizabeth Arredondo MEd, LPC-S

Rights Department, 2442 Michelle Drive, Tustin, CA 92780.

Trilogy Christian Publishing/ TBN and colophon are trademarks of Trinity Broadcasting Network.

For information about special discounts for bulk purchases, please contact Trilogy Christian Publishing.

Trilogy Disclaimer: The views and content expressed in this book are those of the author and may not necessarily reflect the views and doctrine of Trilogy Christian Publishing or the Trinity Broadcasting Network.

Manufactured in the United States of America

10 9 8 7 6 5 4 3 2 1

Library of Congress Cataloging-in-Publication Data is available.

B-ISBN#: 978-1-64773-921-8

E-ISBN#: 978-1-64773-922-5

Dedication

I dedicate this book first to my husband, who never left my side while walking this journey of healing. Second, to my two boys, Azriel and Zayed, for being strong and courageous through this process. And last, to my father, who is now with the Lord, for his unconditional love and prayers.

Contents

Foreword

While faced with a life-threatening disease, Betty overcame in a very positive and joyful journey. She has written an encouraging, uplifting, and incredible book regarding her journey of faith, hope, strength, and courage.

I have had the privilege of knowing Betty for many years and know her to be a woman of grace, joy, and character. Her dedication and commitment to the office she held as a local Aglow International president was extraordinary. While receiving chemotherapy for breast cancer, at times too weak to leave home, she would invite her board members to her home and conduct her board meetings from her bed.

Betty is a perfect example of one who has taken God at His Word, as stated in Isaiah 41:13, "For I, the LORD your God, will hold your right hand, saying to you, 'Fear not, I will help you'"(NKJV). As you read Betty's book, you too will be inspired and receive hope as you learn how she discovered that God is with you, no matter what situation you may encounter.

—Carol Torrance, US Aglow International Director

Introduction

In this book, you will find three tools that are effective to use in your everyday life. They are the powerful Word of God, the voice of praise, and obedience. Illness may attack believers for many reasons, but it is a time of rejoicing because it is when God's power is revealed to the unbeliever and believer alike in a magnificent way. Be not dismayed but rise up and soar with wings like eagles, for this is the time to shine for God. Many times we do not understand why God allows disease and trials to come into our lives. We could be doing everything right but then tragedy hits us. I believe God allows trials to come into our lives for spiritual growth. It is one of the best ways to have to connect with Him at a deeper level.

Some of the things you will read in this book may sound out of the ordinary, but remember, God is in the business of working out of the ordinary. God never intended that we suffer. He took all that with Him on the cross for us. But because we are human and there is still sin in this world, we become distracted, and many times He may use creative ways to grab our attention again. Be careful what you pray for; God will use whatever it takes to get your attention.

I believe the story you are about to read can change your life. Pray and ask God what He wants you to learn from this book. He is so faithful and perfect that He will show you what it is you need from this book. Go deeper with Him and allow Him to guide you on an adventurous path into

His secret place of redemption. I guarantee you will never want to leave it, and you will never be the same again.

Chapter 1

The Diagnosis

But he answered and said, Every plant, which my heavenly father hath not planted, shall be rooted up. Matthew 15:13 (KJV)

It was May 19, 2005. I had gone to visit my family physician. Later, I expressed a concern to my boss about a ball I had found protruding under my right arm. I shared with her that I was going to be taking a few days off because I was going to Austin, Texas, to see a plastic surgeon about a breast reduction. I had considered having breast reduction surgery for many years but had just never done it. I needed to proceed with that plan because the weight of my breasts was beginning to affect my back. So, as I continued to explain to my boss that I was going to be out of town for a few days, she stopped me and said, "Well, Betty, you need to have that checked. If something is wrong that plastic surgeon is not going to touch you." This conversation alarmed me to the point that I called my husband that same afternoon and shared with him this concern.

My husband, Alex, was a pharmaceutical sales representative at the time and knew many doctors. He also came from a family that had thirteen doctors. He immediately got on the phone and set up an appointment to see my family doctor, who was

Alex's uncle. I went in right away to see Dr. Osio, and I showed him where the ball was. He felt it and proceeded with a breast exam, when he found another lump.

He took my hand and had me feel where the lump was. It was on the right breast. He immediately said, "I am ordering a mammogram and sonogram to see what this may be."

I did not know what to feel or think at that moment. My mind began to recall a friend of mine having a similar bump on her breast. She called me so that I could pray for her. We prayed, and the results came back negative. The doctor told her it was just calcification.

My appointment with Dr. Osio was on a Friday, and on Monday afternoon I went in for both tests. Two days later I was back in the doctor's office for the results of the tests. The doctor said the results looked suspicious, and he was sending me to a surgeon for a biopsy. A few days later I saw the surgeon. While I was in his office, he tried aspirating the protruding ball with a needle in the hope that it would deflate. It was not successful, making the biopsy necessary.

A week later I had the biopsy. I was then told that it would take ten days to get any results back from the lab. For ten days we waited and prayed that everything would be fine. I never once entertained the thought that I might have breast cancer. It never crossed my mind that I was going to have to go down that road. I continued living my happy busy life as though nothing was wrong. Then the day came to see the surgeon for the results. When he came in to see me, he checked my biopsy incision and asked that I get dressed, then he left the room. When this happened my husband said, "This is not good." Working with doctors, day in and day out, he pretty much knew how they operated. He felt something was not right. Sure enough, when the doctor returned, he said, "I don't know how else to tell you except just to tell you straight up. You have stage II breast cancer."

Immediately my husband began to cry. Tears streamed down his face, as though he was saying, "This is not happening." I stood strong and I looked at the doctor in the eye, and I said, "Okay, what is my next step from here?"

The doctor began to reassure me that I was not going to die, and many survive breast cancer very well when it's caught in the early stages. He explained that there are four stages to breast cancer, but if it is caught in stage I or II, chances of survival are much higher. It was a relief to hear that we had caught it early, but at the same time I felt like telling the doctor, "Stop sugar-coating and be real with me." Instead I said: "Doctor, I have a lot of faith in God. I kicked the myasthenia gravis [more on this in chapter 11], I can kick this as well."

The doctor responded, "That's what you need, a positive attitude and much faith and you will do well." Then he proceeded to instruct me that I would need more tests run to confirm the diagnosis.

During this discussion with the doctor, I could see out of the corner of my right eye that my husband was devastated. After visiting with the doctor, Alex hugged me and said, "I will be with you every step of the way."

When we left the doctor's office and were walking to our cars, I stopped in the parking lot, turned to him, and said, "God has a message for me, and we are about to get very serious with Him."

Alex went to work, and I did the same. As I drove back to work, I was alone with God for a few minutes. I began to praise Him for this trial. Tears streaming down my face, I told Him, "I will go through whatever pain I need to for Your glory to be shown through my life. Whatever I go through will not compare to what You did for me on the cross. Lord, I trust You completely and will serve You all the days of my life."

On the way to work, I stopped by my sister's work to see her. I felt I needed family and she was the only one available since my parents were out of town. When I told my sister what my diagnosis was, we began to cry together. Christy is my only sister. We had a brother who died instantly on impact at the age of seventeen in a car accident. Christy is eleven years younger than me and I practically raised her when she was born. I often tell people she was my live human baby doll. At age eleven I would dress her, change her diaper, feed her, and play with her. It was so much fun. That day when I shared with her that I had breast cancer, I realized how much we loved each other and how much life would change for our family if I did not survive.

When I got to work, I told only a few key people what my findings were. One of those key people was Bridgette, my dearest friend I worked with and loved. I thought she was going to have a breakdown when I told her. She took it as hard as my husband did. I was the one telling her God had a plan and He is in control of everything. Everything was going to be all right.

The day continued as if everything was fine. That night I had planned a swimming party for my younger son, Zayed. It was his birthday, and invitations had gone out and party preparations were already in motion. We continued with our plans and had the party. Alex and I pulled it off that night and did not share our findings with anyone. After the party was over, we went home, opened gifts, and went to bed. In bed that night Alex and I hugged each other tight and cried for about fifteen minutes. I expressed my fear to him, and he said he could not live without me and that he was going to do everything possible to get the best medical care for me. We went to sleep that night asking God to spare my life. I had two children to finish raising and still had a mission to complete.

The next morning, we went to church. The praise and worship was powerful that morning. I could feel the presence of God beginning to move. Then the pastor felt led to pray for his wife, who was suffering from a condition called vertigo. He laid hands on her and we all agreed with him in prayer. He then felt led to pray for those who were sick. I must have looked like I thought I was on *The Price Is Right* because I almost ran to the altar. The anointing was so strong that I fell to my knees, crying and praying for a touch from heaven. Just the thought of leaving my small children behind devastated me. I did not want to die.

The pastor began laying hands on people. When he laid hands on me, I fell flat on my back under the power of the Holy Spirit. I always tell people that when this happens, let God speak to you. He wants to talk to you. That morning the Lord spoke to me and He said, "I will heal you, but you will minister for Me."

I responded, "Yes, Lord."

Shortly after this word from God the healing process began. From that moment on I dove into the Scriptures and stood on the healing promises of God. Psalm 118:17 (KJV) says, "I shall not die, but live, and declare the works of the LORD." Matthew 15:13 (KJV) says, "Every plant, which my heavenly father hath not planted, shall be rooted up." I knew God had not planted this cancer and I believed He was going to uproot it completely. First Corinthians 15:26–27 (KJV) says, "The last enemy that shall be destroyed is death. For he hath put all things under his feet. But when he saith all things are put under him, it is manifest that he is excepted, which did put all things under him." These are a few of many Scriptures I read over and over.

I now had a word from God. He said He was going to heal me, I just had to minister for Him. And I said "Yes Lord." From the time I was in my mother's womb God had a call on my life (more on this in chapter 10). He had been asking me to minister for Him for many years and I was, as I was serving in my church, but God wanted something more from me. I remember feeling unsure of what God wanted me to do for Him and at the same time excited to see Him work in my life.

Reflection Questions

1. Where does your faith go when you receive bad news?

2. What do you do when God gives you a word? Has He given you a word lately?

Chapter 2

The Second Opinion

"Well, we have the best physician in the world." Dad

Since the results were positive, my surgeon ordered more tests. At that point, my husband felt it was necessary to go directly to MD Anderson Cancer Center in Houston. At the time, we lived about a six-hour drive from the facility, but Alex felt it was best to get the second opinion from them. My surgeon had set up a battery of tests to be run at a local hospital, but we opted to cancel the test and instead go have them done at MD Anderson Cancer Center.

Shortly after canceling my appointment at our local hospital, I received a phone call from a cousin who worked there. She had seen my appointment scheduled and canceled and become alarmed. I explained to her that we were going to go straight to MD Anderson Cancer Center for a second opinion and there they would run all the tests needed.

I asked her to please refrain from sharing these findings with anyone in our family because I had not told my parents yet. My parents were out of town and were not getting back for another four days. I wanted to make sure they found out about my condition from me and no one else. My cousin assured me she would not share the news with anyone. I come from a huge Hispanic family and I knew news like this would spread like wildfire. I did not want my parents to hear about it while on their vacation.

A few days later my parents returned from their trip. When they arrived, Alex and I picked them up from the bus station and took them out for breakfast. At breakfast we shared the news. They are such people of prayer that their reaction was calm, and I will never forget what my father said to me that morning. He was a very meek man of few words, but that morning he said, "Well, we have the best physician in the world." And with those words of hope we began to pray for a miracle.

Soon after, we began the process of getting an appointment with MD Anderson Cancer Center. Everyone we spoke to told us it would take a very long time to get an appointment. Alex, being the computer-savvy person that he is, went online and filled out a self-referral application. The form read that someone would contact us within ten days of submitting the referral. Day nine came around and no one had contacted us. Alex called, and at that very moment someone canceled their appointment, making a slot available for me to see a doctor. We were so thankful to God, knowing well that He works all things together for good.

Our journey to Houston the first time was a tough one. There were so many tests to be run. I endured test after test for two days. I was tired and Alex was tired, and nervous as well because he wanted to make sure he understood everything that was going on. My mother was with us and she was tired. This trip was the first of many to come. It was common for us to make the six-hour drive to Houston, stay overnight, return home the day after our appointments, arrive home at midnight, and go to work the next day. Alex and I managed to maintain our jobs through this crisis. It was evident that God's supernatural strength was with us.

After much testing, the doctor's second opinion was that I did indeed have stage II breast cancer of the right breast. They proceeded to explain that every case is unique, and every plan of treatment is individual. My treatment was going to consist of chemotherapy, surgery, and possible radiation. Since the cancer had already spread to one of the lymph nodes, the chemotherapy was going to be more aggressive.

Shortly after receiving the results, my journey towards recovery began. The doctors prescribed twelve cycles of chemo to start with. The first step was to have a port-a-cath inserted on my left side. This device is used to inject the chemo directly into an artery, which then immediately goes into your system. Chemo is a powerful drug that kills cancer, but it also comes with side effects. Many patients experience pain, discomfort, extreme weight loss or weight gain, nausea, vomiting, weakness, and much more. My experience was different because the power of God was with me every step of the way. The only side effect I felt from those first twelve cycles was tiredness. Every time I had a chemo treatment I would have to come home and rest for the remainder of that day.

The port-a-cath surgery was traumatic for me. I remember sitting in the prep bed in the hospital waiting to be taken in for surgery, and I just began to cry. I didn't understand why I was crying because I was not afraid of the cancer; the Lord had already given me a word that He was going to heal me. And my husband was lovingly holding my hand, caressing my face, and kissing me on my forehead, telling me he loved me. I think two things were happening. One was the love in that room was overwhelming. God was using my husband to channel His love toward me. The second thing was the mere fact that having that port-a-cath inserted marked the beginning of a long journey toward healing. The reality of that happening began to hit me hard. I did not fear the cancer, but I feared the side effects of the chemo. This is when my family went into a season of diligent prayer and fasting for me.

Reflection Questions

1. When trauma hits your life, what is the first thing you think about?

2. What does God want you to know when you are in the middle of a difficult decision or event in your life?

Chapter 3

The Forty-Day Prayer Vigil

From the very onset of this prayer vigil God began His healing process in me.

It was Father's Day weekend, and in my parents' church they have a tradition of taking the fathers out for dinner. On Saturday evening I was invited to join the church tradition and go out for dinner with them. At the restaurant, as we were waiting to be served, one of my aunts suggested having a forty-day prayer vigil in my honor asking God for a miracle. This idea took off with zeal because I come from a family that believes strongly in fasting and prayer.

I had an aunt, Tia Rosa, who left a legacy of fasting and prayer. She is now with the Lord, but when she was alive, she always prayed for people. When Tia Rosa heard that someone in the family was sick, she would get in her car and drive to their home and personally pray for them, asking God to heal them from all ailments. She had such love and faith in God that she just had to spread it everywhere she went. On numerous occasions when family members had fatal conditions, she would start a forty-day prayer vigil for that family member and would fast for God to move and heal. My family has received many miracles because of this faith.

That night when the suggestion was given, the family agreed that this is what God wanted from us. The prayer vigil began in this little church named Rios de Agua Viva. This was the church that my tia Rosa had built years ago, before she went to be with the Lord. It was her dream and vision to have a church built on the family land inherited by her parents. With my family's history of miracles, it seemed only right to start this prayer vigil. Almost fifty years prior, my uncle Felix, the youngest of thirteen brothers and sisters, was healed of myasthenia gravis, an incurable disease. Neither of my grandparents was a Christian during the time when he was sick. Back in those days, treatment for myasthenia gravis was not as advanced as it is now. My grandparents would take my uncle up to Temple, Texas, for treatment at Scott & White hospital. The last time he was taken to Scott & White for treatment, the doctors sent him home to die, for they had done all they could for him. My grandparents and a few of his siblings took my uncle to a boardinghouse for the night after receiving the bad news. The story told to me and all my family is that an evangelist was staying at the boardinghouse that same night. When the lady of the home got my uncle and everyone settled for the night, the evangelist asked what was wrong with my uncle. The question arose after seeing my uncle being carried in by his brother to lay him on a bed in the room where they would be housed for the night. I am told that my uncle was very thin and not able to walk, as myasthenia gravis will make you very weak and unable to hold your body up on your own. The evangelist asked the lady of the house if she thought they would allow him to pray for him. She asked my grandparents if they would like this man of God to pray for their son. They immediately agreed, for they were desperate for a miracle. The evangelist prayed for my uncle and led them all in the prayer of salvation that night. That night my grandmother gave her life wholeheartedly to

Jesus, believing in a miracle and promising to change her life forever if He would heal her son.

The next morning, the lady of the boardinghouse got up early to cook breakfast for all her guests. Suddenly she saw my uncle walk into the kitchen asking for food, for he was hungry. She raised her hands in the air, praising and thanking God, for a miracle had taken place before her very eyes. My uncle had not been able to walk or eat, and that morning he walked on his own and asked for food. The family woke up as they heard all the commotion. The evangelist had already left the boarding-house early that morning for he'd had to get on the road. That miracle changed my family from that day forward. Since then, my family has believed in praying for miracles. My grandparents dedicated their lives to God the rest of their days. They were so grateful for the miracle. My uncle is alive and well today and became a minister, preaching the gospel wherever he is given an open door.

From the very onset of our forty-day prayer vigil God began His healing process in me. We would meet every night at 7 p.m. without fail to pray for my healing. As the extended family heard about the prayer vigil they would come whenever they could to pray. Others in need would come for prayer as well. Many were healed and some even received Jesus as their Savior. It is amazing how Jesus works in the midst of people seeking Him.

Reflection Questions

1. What is your thought on fasting and praying for a miracle?

2. Do you believe God can give you a miracle in your life today?

Chapter 4

Mustard Seed Faith

Because of your little faith. For truly, I say to you, if you have faith like a grain of mustard seed, you will say to this mountain, "Move from here to there," and it will move, and nothing will be impossible for you. Matthew 17:20 (ESV)

Matthew 17:20 talks about having faith as a mustard seed. The story begins with verse 14 where a man came to Jesus and begged Him to have mercy on his son who was epileptic. This father asked Jesus to heal his son because he had gone to his disciples and they had prayed for him, but the son did not heal. Jesus exhorted the disciples and said to them: "O faithless and perverse generation, how long shall I be with you? how long shall I bear with you?" Matthew 17:17 (ASV). Then Jesus rebuked the demon out of the son and healed him. The disciples asked Jesus why they could not cast that demon out of this boy and Jesus answered, "Because of your little faith. For truly, I say to you, if you have faith like a grain of mustard seed, you will say to this mountain, 'Move from here to there,' and it will move, and nothing will be impossible for you" (Matthew 17:20 ESV). This verse captured my attention in a profound way. First you must believe with all your heart, and second, you must have the faith of a mustard seed.

When the Lord revealed this Scripture to me, He impressed on me to go to the grocery store and buy some mustard seed. I sent my husband to buy it for me and when I first saw it, I placed it in my hand and said, "We are calling this mustard seed faith."

I was so impressed by how small it was in appearance that I had a creative idea on how I could share it with others. I decided to get some little plastic ziplock bags and put one mustard seed in each one. On the outside of the ziplocks I placed labels that my husband helped create. The labels said *MSF Matt. 17:20*. MSF stood for Mustard Seed Faith. These little ziplocks with one mustard seed in them were shared at an annual Aglow retreat. At the retreat one mustard seed was placed in each one of the women's hands so that everyone could feel the seed.

If you have never seen what a mustard seed looks like, you need to see one and touch one. As I share this Mustard Seed Faith with others, I tell them that is all God expects from us. And with this faith He will move mountains. Your mountain could be in your finances, in your physical body, or in your emotional being. He is your heavenly Father and He wants to give you miracles. He wants to bless you financially and He wants to heal you emotionally. He says in verse 21, "However, this kind does not go out except by prayer and fasting" (NKJV). Here we are instructed to pray and fast to receive miracles. In my case I was asking God to heal me from breast cancer, and through His Word He was asking my family and me to fast.

Soon after we began the 40 days of prayer my family began to fast. I could not fast as they did because I was under chemo treatment, but God began to show me that my eating habits needed to change.

Reflection Questions

1. Do you believe God wants to give miracles to you?

2. What does Mustard Seed Faith mean to you?

Chapter 5

Change of Diet

I shall not die, but live, and declare the works of the LORD.
Psalm 118:17 (KJV)

Along with prayer and Scripture, the Lord began to direct me into a radical diet and show me through literature and knowledgeable people how to care for my body and what supplements to take. God in His ultimate wisdom knew what my body needed to restore it to health.

I radically changed my diet, to where 75 percent of my food was raw. I ate no refined sugar or white flour because I learned that these two things feed the free radicals in your body that in turn feed cancer cells. I drank at least eight glasses of water a day, and I took immune- boosting and antioxidant supplements to strengthen my immune system to help fight the disease.

Norman Vincent Peale once said, "Stand up to your obstacles and do something about them. You will find that they haven't half the strength you think they have." I stood up to my obstacle with full force and found it had no strength.

Many times we provoke our bodies into the diseases we have

because we are not eating properly. God created good food for good nutrition. He knew what our bodies would need to function properly. Let us remember He was the designer of our internal bodies as well as our external bodies. Modern foods contain ingredients that are not natural and that, once put into our bodies, cause our bodies to react in the form of disease. God was beginning to show me that I needed to cleanse my body.

I was taken to a nutritionist that really helped guide me as to what to eat and what not to eat. She told me to take flaxseed oil capsules daily. She also instructed me to give myself enemas to help cleanse my colon. She was a firm believer that disease starts in the colon because we neglect to cleanse it. I remember hearing stories from my mother and other ladies of how their mothers made them drink castor oil from time to time to cleanse their system. I do not know how but somewhere we lost that instruction because I do not remember having to do that as a little girl.

I must give a disclaimer: I am not a medical doctor nor a nutritionist, but I am simply sharing the journey God led me through to restore my health and heal me from breast cancer. How He instructs others may be different because we are all individuals and are uniquely designed by Him and He knows what we need.

Along with the flaxseed oil capsules I was also taking a product called Juice Plus. This product has been approved by the FDA as a food, not as a food supplement. It comes in capsule form and, when taken daily, will give you the same nutrition as though you were eating seventeen different fruits and vegetables. I believe we do not get the required nutrition from our foods today. I know I was not and that is why when I was introduced to this product, I signed up to take it. I know it played an important part in my road to healing because fruits and vegetables are what contain the antioxidants needed to fight against the free radicals that feed cancer cells.

After five weeks of chemo, it was time to return to MD Anderson for a follow-up visit. I was given a sonogram on the right breast and lymph node. That morning I asked the Lord, "What will they find in that sonogram?" and I heard an inner voice I believe was the Lord say, "*Nothing.*" Praise God!

After the sonogram I waited to hear from the doctor, and soon he came in and said, "Your body has responded well to the chemo. When you first came to us your lymph nodes were covered in cancerous tumors, but they have all dissolved and there are no more tumors."

My heart jumped for joy. I could not contain myself. God had performed another miracle in my life. Praise God, I will forever declare His works because I shall live and not die! Just like it reads in Psalm 118:17: "I shall not die, but live, and declare the works of the Lord" (KJV). This Scripture became one of my favorites after reading Dodie Osteen's book *Healed of Cancer*. This book has been deeply inspirational, and since I have read it, I have given many copies away to others who are battling cancer. Dodie Osteen was healed of cancer of the liver because she spoke the powerful Word of God over her body daily. God's Word heals in a powerful way. It penetrates in one's soul, heart, and mind. Then it manifests in the healing of the physical body.

Though the cancerous tumors were gone, doctors felt it would be best that I continue with the remaining seven chemo treatments. I did not understand why but I was obedient and accepted the treatment. If you have never had chemo or been in someone's life who has had to go through it, it is a difficult process to endure. Once a week I reported to the oncology clinic where a needle was inserted into my port-a-cath. The needle was hooked up to an IV filled with a chemo cocktail created by my MD Anderson doctors. I was seated in a room filled with reclining chairs occupied by many others receiving chemo treatments as well. The treatment is set up in a way that it drips for five or six hours into your bloodstream. It cannot flow any faster because the chemo is typically too strong and the body needs time to adjust to it. It is a long process that leaves one drained for a couple of days. I remember taking chemo treatments on Fridays so that I had Saturday and Sunday to recuperate before heading back to work on Monday.

Many times, after chemo treatments, I would spend Friday afternoons with my boys sitting on my bed by my side. I was too weak to go to the dinner table so they would sit in bed with me and talk to me or do homework. We would watch movies together. My boys were very close to me then, as they are now. Both of my boys went to a Christian school for their elementary years. Prayer requests in school were not uncommon. My youngest would request prayer at school every morning for his mommy that was sick with cancer. When the boys would come home from school, they would go straight to my bedroom to check on me and ask me if I needed anything. I felt so blessed to have my children with me one more day. My heart was so grateful each and every day God gave me just to be alongside my family.

After these treatments were completed it was time to return to MD Anderson for another follow-up visit with the doctor. Another sonogram was performed and again the doctor said there were no cancerous tumors. Everything looked good but it was a real disappointment to learn that I was going to have to undergo four more chemo treatments once every three weeks. This was the second phase of chemo. These treatments are much stronger and harder on the body. Well, again I prayed: "Lord, I will submit and be obedient and take these chemo treatments." I felt the Lord spoke to my heart and said, "You will go through the whole process so that you may understand others that go through this kind of healing process." When I realized what God was doing in me, I felt disappointed that I was going to have to go through all this suffering, but at the same time I felt excited about what God was going to do in me and through me.

Reflection Questions

1. Has there ever been a time in your life when you felt disappointed but you knew God was still in that situation?

2. Write about what you learned about what God was showing you during that time. Perhaps God was healing a part of you that needed to be healed.

Chapter 6

Aglow

And the peace of God, which passeth all understanding, shall keep your hearts and minds through Christ Jesus. Philippians 4:7 (KJV)

In the middle of this process of healing, I was invited to help start a new Aglow chapter in one of our local cities. Aglow International is a trans-denominational organization of Christian men and women with more than four thousand local groups in 170 nations of the world. It is one of the largest international women's organizations with over twelve hundred local groups in the US alone. Aglow reaches an estimated 17 million men and women each year through local groups. Its mission is to help restore and mobilize men and women around the world, to promote gender reconciliation in the body of Christ as God designed, and to amplify awareness of global concerns from a biblical perspective.

It is an awesome organization that helps connect men and women to God all over the world. I was first exposed to this ministry as a sixteen-year-old. My mother was a pioneer in starting a Spanish chapter in our hometown of McAllen, Texas, thirty-nine years ago. She has been a part of Aglow for that many years and at the time was on the area board for our region. It is wonderful how God uses different vehicles to heal us. Thirty-nine years ago, when my mother first started the Spanish Aglow chapter, she was going through a period of grief over the loss of my brother, who was killed in a car accident at the age of seventeen. My family was devastated. But through this ministry God began a work of healing in my mother's life. Many came to know the Lord through this ministry while she was grieving the loss of her one and only son. Many miracles and prophecies came forth. God was bringing His healing and making many whole again. I learned through my mother's experience and then through my cancer how God will never waste your pain. It is through pain that we grow and mature. He never said we would not suffer but He did say He would never leave us or forsake us. It is funny how the legacy is passed on because I truly feel God used Aglow to begin the healing of my emotions and mind, resulting in the physical healing of my breast cancer.

In May of 2005 I received a phone call from Soco Chavez, the Aglow area officer who oversaw starting new chapters at that time. She asked if I would attend a meeting at her house concerning starting a new chapter. I said I would help but I could not oversee anything because my family and my job kept me very busy. She said no problem, just come to the meeting. I attended the meeting several times, and as I prayed for this new chapter the Lord began to work in my heart about getting involved. I kept resisting the commitment, but God kept tugging at my heart. While this was happening, I had not been diagnosed with breast cancer yet. Later, when I was given the diagnosis, I understood why I felt the tug in my heart so strong to be a part of Aglow. The Lord had already told me that He would heal me, but I needed to minister for Him. Aglow presented an open door for ministry.

During our planning stages in working with the Aglow ladies on the board I kept saying I was willing to take a leadership position, but I did not want to be the president. I felt it was too much responsibility to have while having to deal with all the chemo treatments, doctor appointments, and surgeries. The ladies kept on insisting that I should take that role and Soco felt that I should too. In prayer one day, the Lord spoke to me and said, "You will become the president of this chapter." I responded, "We'll see, Lord," as if I had a choice.

Battling with God did not work, because at our next board meeting with the Aglow ladies, Soco assigned our office positions and it was agreed upon by all members that I become the president of this new chapter. I knew in my heart that God was giving me this position and that I had to be obedient. One major lesson I have learned through this whole experience is that if you are obedient to what God is asking you to do, then He will allow all your desires, needs, and wants to fall into place. It is just like when we negotiate with our children. When my boys were young, when they asked for something they wanted, I would ask them if they had done their chores. When I saw that they had completed their chores then I would say yes to whatever it was they wanted to buy or do. It is the same way with God. Remember, we are His children and He is our father. As our Father He wants to fill our every need and desire, but He expects us to be obedient children, just as we expect obedience from our own children.

Out of obedience, I accepted the office of president with this new Aglow chapter. Once I made the decision, the blessings began to flow. The ladies on my local board were incredibly supportive and awesome. The meetings we had were exciting and a blessing to those that attended. It is amazing what God can do when you are obedient. When you are obedient, God's grace, wisdom, and special favor follow you wherever you go and in whatever you do.

One summer in July we took a family vacation to a nearby island. I call it a vacation, but it really was not a vacation for my husband because he had to work. However, for the boys and me it was a vacation. The boys were out of school and I was off work for the summer as I worked as a school counselor and followed the boys' school schedule. As the days went on, I felt such peace. One morning I sat outside on the balcony enjoying the ocean view and thanking God for His peace in my family. It was such an enjoyable day that I just did not want it to end. I do not recall ever feeling that way since becoming a married woman or even a mother to these two boys. My life felt as though something was always running on empty. Satisfaction with life just was not there. But that morning I felt completely satisfied in God. There was that peace that surpassed all understanding that the Scripture talks about in Philippians 4:7: "And the *peace* of God, which passeth all understanding, shall keep your hearts and minds through Christ Jesus" (KJV, emphasis added). I felt deeply blessed to feel His peace. This was His way of telling me that in my obedience I was completely in His will.

Let me encourage you to pray for peace in your home. God will help you find ways to attract His peace. It is amazing what a difference it makes when your family is at peace with each other. If you are searching for God's peace, be obedient in what He is asking you to do for Him. Your life will change, and you will never be the same again. He is always ready to serve you, but are you ready to serve Him?

Reflection Questions

1. Where is God calling you to be obedient to Him?

2. Do you feel peace in your life in this moment? If not, ask God what you need to do to feel His peace.

Chapter 7

Chemotherapy

*Do not be anxious about anything, but in everything by prayer
and supplication with thanksgiving let your requests be made
known to God. Philippians 4:6–8 (ESV)*

I remember the very first meeting we had as an Aglow chapter.
It was at a pizza place in Edinburg, Texas, on a Saturday morning in October 2005. It was an awesome first meeting. There
was an air of expectancy. We had a full house of ladies excited
to begin a new Aglow chapter.

The day before, I had had a chemo treatment. This chemo
treatment was one of four very strong chemo treatments, and
the side effects were strong as well. The first twelve chemo
treatments were fine. The only side effects I had were hair loss
and tiredness. With the first chemo treatment the Lord taught
me how to pray for my organs through my dear sister Gloria.

One day after one of the prayer vigils, she instructed me to
pray for the chemo. She said, "As you see the chemo coming
into your body, begin to speak to your body and speak to the
chemo. Say: 'Chemo, you will only do what you need to do and
nothing else.' Then you begin to speak to each individual organ
and say: 'Kidneys, you are going through a trauma right now,

but Jesus is right there with you healing you. Do not be afraid; everything will be all right.'"

I prayed this way for each one of my organs: liver, colon, lungs, and stomach. The day before our first meeting I had the first chemo of the second phase of chemo treatments, and I prayed as it was being injected into my veins. I said to it: "Chemo, you will do only what you need to do in my body and nothing else." I spoke to all my organs: "Kidneys, liver, colon, lungs, stomach, you are going through a trauma right now, but Jesus is right there with you and everything is going to be fine." I felt fine until three o'clock the next morning. I began to experience the nausea. At about five o'clock I got up and took a nausea pill, crawled back in bed, and began to pray. I said, "Lord, I have already prayed about this nausea, but now I need Your blood running through my bloodstream, and I need Your immune system to boost my immune system so I can minister for You this morning at the Aglow meeting. Remember it's our first meeting, and remember You put me in this position of president, and I have to be there."

Shortly after I prayed, the nausea began to subside. I was able to run that meeting with no problem at all. God is awesome! It was so incredible how God worked in my body that day. I had just experienced a Matthew 17:20 moment. I saw how having that mustard seed faith moved my mountain. There is such authority in the Word of God that you can speak to your mountain and it will move. God gives us the tools to fight—not to lose but to win. Remember He is a God of excellence and He gives His children the best. He gives you the best positions in leadership, and with leadership comes authority. In the spiritual sense we are all leaders against the wiles of the enemy. Do not let the enemy wipe you out, destroy you, or kill you. Pick up your spiritual tools and fight. Pave the way for others and teach them to fight the spiritual battle against cancer, against financial crisis and emotional bruises. Speak to your soul and say to it: "Rise up, O soul, and be glad, for this is the day the Lord has made and be glad in it. For by His stripes I am healed, and I shall not die but live and declare the works of the Lord, for He is the same yesterday, today and forever. And He will never leave me nor forsake me." Take a hold of your soul and emotions and fight the battle for health.

King David would speak to his soul. Psalm 42:11 says, "Why art thou cast down, O my soul? Why art thou disquieted within me? Hope thou in God; for I shall yet praise him, the help of my countenance, and my God" (ASV).

Tell your soul to submit to the will of God. His will is that you live and be in good health to declare His works. Tell your soul to be obedient to God's will and to rise up and be glad, for this is the day the Lord has made. Remind your soul of Philippians 4:6–8, "Be anxious for nothing, but in everything by prayer and supplication, with thanksgiving, let your requests be made known to God; and the peace of God, which surpasses all understanding, will guard your hearts and minds through Christ Jesus. Finally, brethren, whatever things are true, whatever things are noble, whatever things are just, whatever things are pure, whatever things are lovely, whatever things are of good report, if there is any virtue, if there is anything praiseworthy, meditate on these things" (NKJV).

Pray a prayer of thanksgiving and say, "Father, thank You for this trial because I know Your glory will be shown through this. Thank You for Your peace and Your healing power flowing through my body, making it well every day I live. Thank You for healing me completely and fully."

It is just that simple. God does not expect you to say some big elaborate prayer. Remember He created you. He knows your thoughts, your plans, and every innermost secret thing about you. Keep it simple, show humility before God. Pull out all the stops and watch Him work incredibly in your life. We serve an awesome God and He is ready to heal you. Are you ready for His healing in your life?

As a therapist, I read and study many concepts, and there is one called trauma bonding. Sometimes we bond with our illness because we find comfort in it, especially if we have been ill for a long time. We cannot see ourselves without the pain or illness we have carried around for months or even years. To grow away from bonding with the trauma, we must have faith and begin to see ourselves free from pain, free from cancer or any other illness we are experiencing. The question remains, are you ready to be healed completely from your ailment?

Reflection Questions

1. How has God reveled to you the authority you have against your pain, whether it be in your physical body, emotions, or mind?

2. Does your soul need reminding to rise up? What can you do today to remind your soul to rise up like David did?

Chapter 8

Surgeries

Thank God for wigs!

After completing all my chemo treatments, it was time for surgery. On February 21, 2006, I was checked into MD Anderson hospital to have the first of three surgeries. The first was a mastectomy. My right breast, along with twenty-seven lymph nodes, was removed and sent to the lab to make sure there was no cancer. The reports came back clean. Praise God! There it was, written in black and white that I was cancer free. I believe I am cancer-free forever.

After receiving this news, I checked into MD Anderson on March 14, 2006, for surgery number two. This surgery was one of reconstruction. I had two surgeries within two weeks, but the miraculous thing about it all was that I experienced no pain. Before each surgery I prayed for my body, preparing it for the trauma that it was going to go through. I spoke to each organ and forewarned them what was going to happen to them, reassuring each organ that Jesus would be right there with them. I know many people were praying for me, and I know those prayers were heard because I felt no pain from either one of those surgeries. I remember when I was in a room after this second surgery my parents came to see me. My father asked me if I had any pain. When I responded with a no, he responded, "Thank You, Jesus! I was praying that you would not have any pain."

Through this process God showed me how much my husband loved me because he never left my side. My chemo treatments lasted five to six hours, and there were times that my husband sat right by my side reassuring me that everything was going to be fine. I thank God for a loving and compassionate husband. I thank God for Pastors David and Gloria whom God chose to guide me in the healing process of my soul and spirit through counseling and prayer. They guided me to another level of faith and into kingdom living. My life will never be the same again.

I learned how much my family loved me because they unselfishly gave of their time for forty nights to pray and fast for my healing. I had two sisters-in-law who unselfishly left their homes to come stay with my children while I was in the hospital in Houston. I also have been blessed with wonderful friends that prayed, called, and sent cards of encouragement. I thank God for the church I attended, The Family Church, for their phone calls and prayers. I believe that God was answering prayer because during the first twelve chemo treatments, I never experienced any of the side effects of nausea or vomiting. The only side effect I experienced was the loss of my hair. Thank God for wigs!

I have a couple funny stories involving my wigs. After losing my hair, my husband asked if he could choose one. I said sure, why not? We went to a wig store in Houston after one of my doctor's appointment, and Alex chose a jet-black straight bob with bangs. I was never one to wear bangs because the weather in south Texas is just too hot, and my bangs would curl with the humidity and never stay in place. One time I wore this wig to one of my MD Anderson doctor's appointment. The routine when I got there was to be placed in a wheelchair. The nurse called me an Egyptian princess as she wheeled me to the doctor's office for my checkup. Having fun with the wig was another thing that helped relieve the trauma of having cancer. I believe it does something to the psyche to bring joy into bad situations.

One time, Alex and I were driving somewhere in our Suburban. Alex rolled down the front windows to allow a breeze to push out the hot air accumulated in the truck. As the breeze came in, my wig flew off my head towards Alex. He caught it like a football and said, "My football coaches always said I had good hands." We laughed for a while. Another time, as a career counselor for my district along with two other career counselors, we would collaborate and put together an annual career fair. This career fair was hosted by another high school, and after the event took place we would gather and debrief. As I was walking towards the gym where the event happened, a gust of wind sent my wig flying off my head, and it rolled for a good while on the grass. Thank God no one was out except a grounds person who was too busy cleaning up to notice. I ran after the wig as it rolled on the ground and quickly placed it back on my head. Inside I was laughing, and when I shared what happened with my colleagues, we laughed together for a good while. I learned that the joy of the Lord comes to us in many ways, even in losing wigs.

After my first surgery, I had to stay in Houston for ten days because we were waiting to see the lab report results on the mass on my right breast and the lymph nodes that were removed. During that time, my husband put me and my mother up in a nice hotel. When he returned to work, my mother stayed with me and we had a great time together as recovery days flew by. The first day I arrived at the hotel a flower arrangement arrived from my church back home. I was so amazed at the details God takes care of because in the arrangement was one of my favorite flowers. I love calla lilies and this arrangement had them. They were so beautiful. I remember asking how they knew. As I asked that question, I felt in my heart God was saying, "Because they were from Me."

A few days later one of my husband's cousins that lived in Houston at the time came to visit me at the hotel. When my mom opened the hotel door, she came in with a vase filled with yellow roses. Yellow roses are also a favorite flower of mine. I could not believe how detailed God was. He remembered what flowers were my favorite and sent them to me through His messengers, who did not even know they were being used by Him as messengers of His awesome love. I remember asking Alex's cousin: "How did you know that my favorite flowers are yellow roses?" And she answered: "I didn't! I just thought they looked bright and cheery!" I was so blessed by those two floral arrangements. I marveled at God's love and His ability to know us in detail.

My last surgery was performed on June 8, 2006. This one was not as bad as the first two. It was a nipple reconstruction and required only one overnight stay in the hospital. I remember waking up from that surgery in immense pain that lasted only a few minutes. I believe God allowed me to feel it for a moment only to let me feel what He was saving me from, because the other two surgeries were absolutely pain free. What I felt for just a few minutes was so painful I cannot imagine what it would have been like had I experienced that type of pain with the other surgeries. God's miraculous ways continue to amaze me.

Reflection Questions

1. Do you find joy in uncomfortable situations? Think of a time when joy came to you and you received it or rejected it because of your suffering.

2. What does the joy of the Lord mean to you?

Chapter 9

Communion and Counseling Sessions

He was wounded for our transgressions, he was bruised for our iniquities; the chastisement of our peace was upon him, and with his stripes we are healed. Isaiah 53:5 (ASV, emphasis added)

During chemotherapy treatments, I continued to receive my healing from Jesus. Every night before I went to bed, I would close my eyes and visualize Jesus on the cross. I communed with Him and I remembered His body that was broken for me. I remembered the blood that was shed for me. I remembered Isaiah 53:5, "He was wounded for our transgressions, he was bruised for our iniquities; the chastisement of our peace was upon him, and with his stripes we are *healed*" (ASV, emphasis added). Then I thanked Him for all my infirmities that He bore, for every stripe He took so that I might be healed. I thanked God for loving me this much. These instructions to commune with God daily for my healing came from Pastors David and Gloria. I did not know this then but now as a professional licensed therapist, I often help people use a visualization technique to find their healing. I am amazed at how God was preparing me through my healing days for my future career as a licensed professional counselor.

One Sunday morning as we took communion, I found myself in a dilemma deciding whether I should take communion or not because I was taught that if you were not in good standing toward a brother or sister, communion should not be taken until reconciliation took place. At that time, my husband and I were not in a good place with each other and I felt terrible, but at the same time I understood that God wanted to continue healing my body. I was also taught that taking communion is good for healing. It represents Jesus giving His life to give us life. As I stood there and as the elements were being passed around, I felt a strong urge to take communion that morning regardless of my circumstances and how I was feeling. I remember crying out to God to forgive me for being at odds with my husband. I asked that we reconcile and be at peace with one another. As I prayed, I remember telling the Lord that I was going to take communion because I needed healing in my body, and I knew that there was power in taking communion. The power in communion comes from understanding what Jesus did on that cross for us. As Jesus suffered on that cross for me and shed His blood for me, He was then covering ground so that I might receive healing now.

As we take communion, we must understand it is out of obedience and remembrance of Him. As we commune with Him in this way, it opens the door for Him to come heal our physical bodies, emotions, hearts, souls, and minds. Jesus always makes a way for our healing if we only believe and don't waver. If we only commit to staying strong and true to Him. The Word teaches us we will always have healing in every area of our lives.

With the prayer vigil in full swing, I sought counseling, taking much of it from Pastors David and Gloria. These wonderful servants of God were placed in my life to lead me to find healing, not just in the physical but in my soul. God used them to teach me how to heal from within first. (Note: Pastors David and Gloria were the pastors of the church left behind by my tia Rosa. It was our family church.)

I had no idea what God had in store for me. As He began to heal my body, He also began healing my past hurts. He began to heal the wounds of my past. In counseling sessions with Pastors David and Gloria, God began to reveal where the wounds began and started healing deep inside me. I began to understand how God does not want us to live in our past, but He desires we live in the present.

I began to understand what it meant to connect with God again. I had always lived for God but because the scars of past hurts were so deep, God could not reach me at that deeper level where He needed me to be. Through much counseling and prayer God delivered my resentful and angry heart to a place of forgiveness and freedom.

When God frees your heart from yourself you begin to see things His way, not yours. As humans we tend to think our own way and develop our own perspective of what is really happening around us. We dream up things that are just not true. Satan has been playing this game in our minds for centuries, but God has a better way to think. Remember in Philippians 4:8 how he talks about "whatever things are true, whatever things are noble, whatever things are just, whatever things are pure, whatever things are lovely, whatever things are of good report, if there is any virtue and if there is anything praiseworthy—meditate on these things" (NKJV). If we can put into action what Philippians 4:8 says, we have mastered our crisis. Whether it is a crisis that requires physical healing, a financial blessing, or emotional healing, this Scripture says it all. Let's not fight against our solution or justify our actions but let's learn to put the Word of God in action in our lives and watch Him heal our physical bodies and our emotions, and supply financial blessings.

Forgiveness is key when needing physical healing. Forgiveness is an action God has given us to free us from anger, resentment, and hurt. Many times, we bottle up our anger, which starts the process of resentment and bitterness. Jesus forgave those who crucified Him. He expects us to forgive those who hurt us. We have a free will and can choose to dwell in our bitterness and resentment. On the other hand, our free will can choose to forgive those who hurt us and bless them. Pray a blessing over their lives and in doing so you begin to release forgiveness, and the blessing of God beyond measure comes to your life in ways you never imagined.

Obedience is another key factor in healing. As we obey God and do what He is asking us to do for Him, He begins the healing process in our body. It is so important to connect with Him and hear what He is saying. We get so caught up with our lives that we do not stop to hear what He wants to say to us. Stop right now and do the following exercise.

Close your eyes. See Jesus. Picture Him (visualize). Tell Him you love Him. Listen to what He is saying to you. Receive His words of encouragement, comfort, or instruction. Allow His presence to heal you from the inside out. Thank Him for His amazing love. Tell Him you will be obedient and that you trust Him. Now open your eyes.

This may sound very strange to some. But we must find that connection with God. We must take time out to visit with Him. He desires our company. He desires to commune with us. He desires that we enter that secret place with Him where only you and He know what is being said. He desires that we make a connection with Him daily. As you begin to make this connection with Him, your desire to connect with Him will increase. Then your relationship with Him will become priority.

Trusting Jesus is also key to your healing. We must trust Him with all our heart, mind, and soul. Proverbs 3:5–6 says, "Trust in the LORD with all thine heart; and lean not unto thine own understanding. In all thy ways acknowledge him, and he shall direct thy paths" (KJV). The Word tells us to trust Him and if we do, He will direct our paths. We may not always understand what He is doing, but rest assured He will always work on your behalf.

You may be thinking, "Betty, you got breast cancer. How's that working in your behalf?" My response is that this disease was meant to kill and destroy me, but God allowed it to happen to open an opportunity for me to see His miraculous power in my life once again in the most awesome way possible. As you begin to trust Him, then and only then will you begin to see miracles happen right before your very eyes. God's amazing love for you will become more evident to you than ever before. His grace will become more than enough. You will begin to feel satisfied with life. Remember He created us, and we have a built-in love bank that only He can fill, and when He does, we can love others. Through His love He heals us so that we can share His love with others. What an awesome way to live.

Understanding how to love one another is the hardest thing to learn. We are so full of selfish reactions instead of understanding and patience. When someone comes at you in reaction mode and says hurtful things, learn to respond quietly. In my field of mental health, I have learned that when someone says hurtful things, it means their brain is dysregulated. If we can just learn to give grace in those moments and not engage with responses of rebuttal but rather allow our brain to stay regulated, then the other person can borrow from our regulated brain and allow the dysregulated brain to become regulated. It is amazing how God created us to help each other even when we are dysregulated. Amazing how allowing God's grace to regulate a dysregulated brain enables the emotional storm to fade. It will soon pass and when it does, results are more peaceful. This happens when one chooses to respond in quietness versus anger. Practice riding out the storm instead of fighting it. The results will surprise you. Ask the Holy Spirit for guidance and help in the middle of the storm. Listen to what He is saying to you. I guarantee He will give instructions that will solve any problem you may encounter better than you could ever do.

I remember one incident when my husband was upset with me for some misunderstanding we had. My normal response was to pull away from him and not talk to him. That night I was serving my boys dinner and I heard the Spirit of God tell me, "Serve your husband." In the past when my husband and I were at odds with each other, I would isolate myself and not even get close to him. This time I obeyed God and served him dinner in bed because he happened to be watching TV in our bedroom. When I walked in with dinner, he looked at me, surprised, and asked, "Are you talking to me now? I thought you had forgotten about me and I am sorry. I did not mean to hurt you."

When God instructs you to do something you normally would not do, chances are He is right on the money about what the outcome will be. He knows each one of us so well. In this instance He knew how my husband would react to the simple act of kindness of serving him dinner in bed. We must learn to hear Him. If we listen, He will get us out of negative situations and into positive ones.

Reflection Questions

1. What does communion mean to you?

2. Has there ever been a time when God spoke to you and asked you to do something? Did you obey? If so, write about how that felt. If not, write about how *that* felt.

Chapter 10

My Birth

For you formed my inward parts; you covered me in my mother's womb. I will praise You, for I am fearfully and wonderfully made; marvelous are Your works, and that my soul knows very well.
Psalms 139:13–14 (NKJV)

I have been told that my birth was one of much travail. My mother was in labor for three days. I was born in 1964, and in those days C-sections were not done as commonly as they are now. My mother suffered much pain in giving birth to me for I was a breach baby.

There was a moment during the labor that my mother stopped groaning from the pain. At that very moment, my father and grandmother were waiting outside the delivery room because in those days no one was allowed in the delivery room as they are today. When my mother went silent and no baby cry filled the room, my grandmother and father held hands, dropped to their knees in front of the door, and began to pray for our lives. Soon after they prayed, they heard the doctor spank my bottom. At first there was no cry and they heard the second spank on the bottom, then the cry was heard. This was a miracle in more ways than one. It was a known fact that my grandmother and my father did not see eye to eye on much of anything—except one thing. They saw eye to eye on love. Love for my mother and the child she bore, but above all love for God. I marvel at how God brought together two people who did not like each other, and in that act of togetherness He brought forth life with a cry. A baby crying for her life, and that baby was me. One can say I have been crying for my life since birth, and every time I cry, Jesus meets me there and gives me more life. I am grateful for His kindness towards me.

I was born the color purple due to a lack of oxygen to my brain. From my mother's womb, God was calling me to serve Him in a special way. From the womb He spared my life and breathed His life into me so that I may live, and not die, to declare His wonderful works (Psalm 118:17). Psalm 139:13–14 says, "For you formed my inward parts; you covered me in my mother's womb. I will praise You, for I am fearfully and wonderfully made; marvelous are Your works, and that my soul knows very well" (NKJV). This Scripture defines my life. The Lord covered me while in my mother's womb for such a time as this. Jesus was there with me in that trauma of struggling to be born. Since before I was born, God had a purpose for my life.

Life is a journey and it is all about what we do for God during that journey. If we could just learn that this life is about serving Him and not ourselves, then fulfillment, happiness, and satisfaction would come. Our greatest moments will always be the ones when we're serving God. We can serve God as we live our everyday lives. Some believe that you must preach, teach, and heal in a church setting to serve God. That is not the only way or place we can be used by Him. It is all about serving Him in your workplace, as you grocery shop, in the doctor's office, at your children's school activities, wherever you find an opportunity to share kindness or give a comforting word or act of service. We live in such a selfish world rather than a selfless world. If we truly follow Jesus' example, we will live selflessly. We would live our lives finding ways to bring others closer to God and sharing the secret to success, fulfillment, and happiness, which is serving Him with all our hearts, passionately in love with Him.

Reflection Questions

1. Is God calling you to minister for Him?

2. Where can you commit to minister for God?

Chapter 11

Myasthenia Gravis

It was just a horrible feeling of not being in control of my body.

Ever since I was born, Satan has been trying to end my life. First it was surviving birth, and later I was involved in multiple car accidents. Thank God for His protection and His Word that never fails.

After having my second son, I began experiencing a lot of fatigue. One Saturday I slept in while my husband took care of my two sons, who were four and one at the time. I did not wake up until two that afternoon. I was so fatigued and really did not know what was going on with my body. Being the wise man that he is, my husband suggested that I see a doctor. I took his suggestion and went to my primary doctor. He took bloodwork and found that I had hypothyroidism. This explained the fatigue and hair loss I had been experiencing. A few months later I began experiencing that fatigue again, but it was only happening in the evenings. Again, I saw a doctor and he could not pinpoint what I had.

Around this time, my husband's grandfather died, and we went to the funeral service. After the burial, the family gathered for a meal and fellowship at my husband's aunt's home. That evening I began getting symptoms again. This time it required two people to walk me to my car. It was embarrassing because it looked as though I was drunk. That evening my husband practically carried me to our bedroom, and later while he was putting the boys to bed, I fell to floor. It was as though my legs gave out completely. He heard my scream and quickly came to my aid. As he picked me up from the floor my body slithered through his hands and I fell to the floor again. It was a scary feeling because I had no control of my body and my speech was slurred. It was so strange. I felt so tired and was not able to get up on my own. This alarmed my husband and he quickly called my mother to come stay with the boys so he could take me to the hospital.

On the way to the hospital he called his uncle, Dr. Osio, who was our primary doctor, and informed him we were on the way to the hospital. When we arrived at the hospital, Dr. Osio and his wife, Letty, along with his uncle Ernest and his wife, Argie, were there waiting for us. We were so relieved to see them. We had no idea what was going on. That night I was admitted to the hospital. Many tests were ordered, trying to find a diagnosis, but they could not find anything wrong with me. The test results showed that I was a little low in iron, vitamin D, and calcium. There was nothing major that stood out.

After three days, I was released from the hospital and I went back to work. I continued with symptoms and still no diagnosis of what I had. I went to Dr. Osio for a follow-up and he said he was not very happy with the results from the hospital. He felt I might have a rare disease called myasthenia gravis, but I had to be evaluated by a neurologist. He referred me to a neurologist, who had me do all kinds of movements as part of his evaluation. At the end of his evaluation, he wrote a prescription for the drug Mestinon, used to help control symptoms of myasthenia gravis. I was instructed to take it four times a day.

It was confirmed that I had myasthenia gravis.

I began taking the medicine and noticed an improvement, but on the days I forgot a dose, I noticed a dramatic change in my body. The symptoms would come back. I would feel limp and sluggish. There were times when I needed help getting down from my vehicle and into my home. It was just a horrible feeling of not being in control of my body.

Even though my body was feeling these symptoms, I was able to work as long as I took my medication four times a day. One day a teacher I worked with told me, "You should have my friend pray for you. She has a gift of healing and she lives just down the road from here."

Then she asked, "Would you like me to call her so you can go see her during your lunch hour?"

Desperate to feel better, I accepted the invitation. During my lunch hour, my husband took me to the home of this beautiful woman of God. Her name was Diana Morales. There she ministered to me, assuring me that faith in God is what heals us. She prayed a simple prayer for healing, and I went back to work. That afternoon I worked without symptoms. I noticed my energy was back. I went home after work and threw away all the medicine I had for myasthenia gravis. Since that day I have not had any symptoms, nor have I taken any more medicine for it. God completely healed me. I praise Him with all my heart for He is good!

Reflection Questions

1. Have you ever experienced God's healing power in your life? If so, what did it feel like?

2. Has God healed you in another way than the healing of your body? If so, how did He heal you? If not physical healing, was it emotional or spiritual?

Chapter 12

Victory Comes with the Connection

What is man, that thou art mindful of him? And the son of man, that thou visitest him? Psalm 8:4 (ASV)

Jesus desires for us to be intimate with Him. Many may not know how this happens. It begins with a true relationship. Just as any relationship requires genuineness, so it is with God. You must truly love Him first. In the natural, when a person is in love, they want to spend every moment of the day with the one they love. So it is with God. You may say, "But that's impossible." Scripture talks about being mindful of Him in Psalm 8:4: "What is man, that thou art mindful of him? And the son of man, that thou visitest him?" (ASV) He wants us to think of Him, talk to Him all day long, 24/7. When we speak to Him inwardly no one hears us but Him.

His peace will place you in a capsule of tranquility and love. His love will pour out to you through others. Do you realize that God uses everyone that crosses your path to encourage you, to love you, and to carry you when you are weak? During my time of surgery recovery and chemo days I received get-well cards, phone calls, and gifts of food already prepared for my family. God was pouring His love over me through all these acts of kindness. Let God use you by sending a card, making that phone call, or running a simple errand for someone. Learn to receive God's love as He sends it your way to bless you. For some of us this is hard because you may be the one always giving and receiving. Put your pride aside and receive however God blesses you.

As we allow God's blessing in our lives and commit to connect with Him daily, victory will come and saturate our lives. First Corinthians 15:26–27 says: "The last enemy that will be destroyed is death. For 'He has put all things under His feet'" (NKJV). But when He says all things are put under Him, it is evident that those who put all things under Him can expect miracles.

Do not be afraid! Fear will paralyze you and it will kill you. Overcome fear by saying, "I am weak, but You are strong!" As humans we tend to be impatient and we want instant miracles. But what we do not understand is that God's working away the rough edges in our lives as we go through the process of healing. A pastor once asked the question: "Do you ever wonder why for new believers instant miracles happen? Do you ever wonder why for those of us that have known God for twenty years, sometimes instant healing does not happen?" For believers it requires more faith. It becomes a process that requires more time and more faith. Let your faith ignite victory! Let your faith establish solid healing! Let your faith bring blessing! Give God something to work with.

Victory comes to us in many facets in our lives. While walking this journey, I chose to find victory in everything. Remember the day my husband and I were running an errand together and how my wig blew off my head when he rolled down his window and it flew directly into his hands? We laughed as my husband said, "Thank God I played football and knew how to catch." In that moment I felt victorious in the sense that we could laugh while in the middle of that storm. God will bring moments of joy if you allow Him to. Choose joy over sorrow in the mist of your pain. Again, we have a choice to ride the wave of the storm, trusting God, or fight it with anger and resentment.

Another victorious moment happened one day while at work. Remember after a long Career Day how I went back to reflect on the day with my colleagues and again I lost my wig? And how I quickly ran after it and placed it back on my head before anyone saw? What a moment of awkward laughter I felt there by myself. Then I shared what happened with my colleagues and we had such a joyous time of laughter that day that I walked away feeling once again victorious, proclaiming ground for my healing. God allows moments of victory to happen to remind us how much He loves us. Again, we have a choice in how to handle our pain. I could have picked up my wig and boohooed all the way home. But I chose victory for victory will always win.

In the moments of shock, grief, anger, and pain, every woman should know that Jesus heals breast cancer. May God give you moments of joy in your storm. May His peace engulf your pain. May His healing carry a message of hope, strength, unwavering faith, and unconditional love. May His healing power present itself to you in all facets of your life. God will never waste our pain if we are willing to grow and mature spiritually. He truly gives us a choice. What will you choose? Joy over sorrow? Victory over defeat?

Reflection Questions

1. How do you spend intimate time with God? Or how can you challenge yourself to spend intimate time with God?

2. How do you walk in victory?

About the Author

Three years after my diagnosis, we moved to San Antonio, Texas, having been transferred there by my husband's pharmaceutical company. We fell in love with San Antonio. Soon after our move there we found Community Bible Church. It has been a blessing to be a part of such an amazing church. Both of our boys have now graduated from high school.

One year after moving to San Antonio, my husband's position got cut due to the restructuring of his company. At that time, I was working on getting my professional counseling license. Once I obtained it, I began to work for a company after my school counseling hours. One day driving home and speaking with my husband, I asked him if he would be interested in auditing a billing and coding class to learn the trade. My thought was that one day when I retired from school counseling I would set up my own private practice. My husband ran with this idea. He established our company and began to credential me as a provider for insurance panels. Seven years later, he grew the practice from one therapy room to four and from one therapist to ten.

I am blown away by what God can do. Thank you, Alex, my husband, for committing to this work God gave us, spending countless hours making sure all is in order and that every need is met. I cannot do this work without you. I am blessed to have you in my life, working with you for one purpose, helping others stabilize mental health conditions as God gives us wisdom, strength, and passion for this work.

I am retired now from NEISD with twenty-seven years of educational service. I practice as an LPC-S in our company, Rapha Counseling, and I have been facilitating a trauma and PTSD mental health group at our church for several years. I am excited to see God's work continue as we serve Him in obedience.

This book is written as a testimony of my healing to be shared with others, that they might find encouragement and faith in the healing power of God. If you are reading this book and do not know Jesus as your personal Savior, do not delay any longer. Jesus is calling you and desires a personal relationship with you. If you want to know Jesus more, pray the following prayer and let Him come into your heart. You will have a life-changing experience.

"Jesus, I need You. I confess that I have sinned and believe that You have died on the cross for me. Forgive me of my sins, and Lord, come into my heart and make me whole."

It is that simple! Know that Jesus loves you. The next step for you is to attend a Bible teaching church. This is very important so that you can learn more about Jesus and His way of living. You will not regret the decision you have just made. God bless you!

Acknowledgments

Throughout my journey of disease and recovery, I acknowledge the many people that made this book possible. First, I acknowledge my heavenly Father. Without God, I would not be alive to write this book. Second, I acknowledge my husband for standing by my side every step of the way. Alex, I love you for never giving up on me and for loving me unconditionally. Even with the scars on my body, you still tell me you love me every day.

I acknowledge my children for being courageous and never letting Mommy's condition stop them from continuing their life activities. I acknowledge my parents and sister for always praying for me and standing by my side as I walked through every surgery and at times chemo treatments and doctors' appointments. By publishing this book I honor my father, as he went to be with the Lord in 2016. He always supported the writing and publishing of this book.

I thank God for my in-laws who were there for me in care of my children and in other ways. I thank my aunts, uncles, and cousins who prayed for me diligently, sent me cards, and gave me gifts as an expression of their love. I thank my work family at McAllen Memorial High School for their acts of kindness toward me during this crisis in my life. I thank Bridgette Vieh, one of my dearest friends, who even changed her diet along with me as I walked through this journey. I thank the Edinburg, Texas, local Aglow chapter board for their prayers and the gifts they gave me. I thank my church family at The Family Church for their prayers and love expressed towards me in so many ways.

Lastly, I thank Pastor David and Sister Gloria for taking me through a path of inner healing as they counseled me through my illness. God always knows what we need and will provide everything as we need it. May the Lord bless each one of you with His crowns in heaven.

My youngest son Zayed, myself then my oldest son Azi

My husband and I

The whole family, Zayed, Alex, Azi and me

Resources

The following books were very helpful to me as I walked through this healing process.

Healed of Cancer by Dodie Osteen

The Maker's Diet by Dr. Jordan S. Rubin (770 Northpoint Parkway, Suite 100/MD, West Palm Beach, Fl 33407 Toll Free (866)465-0094 Telephone: (561)472-9277, Fax: (561)492-9296

Website: www.gardenoflifeusa.com

God's Creative Power for Healing by Charles Capps

Website: www.Charlescapps.co